Time
Inspirations II

By
Leonard McNeely

PRESS

Quiet Time Inspirations II
by Leonard McNeely

Printed in the United States of America

ISBN 9781498464390

www.xulonpress.com

To

My wife, my sons, my daughter-in-loves, and my grandchildren.

Thank you for inspiring me to leave a legacy that is eternal

Heartfelt Thanks. . .

To my wife, Kelley, for listening to me and believing in me as I have begun to write and share.

To my daughter-in-love, Julie McNeely, for editing these words so that others can receive the message God has laid on my heart.

To my secretary and family friend, Tammy Frailey, for helping compile these poems at various times to make publication possible.

And most of all, to my Lord and Savior, Jesus Christ, for Your endless love and grace.

I t all started December 2012, as we celebrated Jesus' birth: that was the day that God began to birth these poems through me. For the next 365 days, I woke up at 4:30 am to start my day and have quiet time with the Lord. No matter where I was, every day, I wrote. It wasn't for the purpose of a book, it was just what the Holy Spirit inspired me to do as I spent time in God's presence. My Quiet Time became my writing time. Whether through nature, life experiences, or reading God's Word, the Holy Spirit would guide me to the truth He wanted me to know and ultimately share.

The poems you find here are common and simple- but that is who I am. I am simply husband to Kelley, Father to Keith, Jarrett, and Chad, Father-in-love to Daphne, Julie, and Angela, and Big L to Dustin, Alex, Kobi, Jonathan, Caroline, Kallie, and Reed.

The blessing of this family has given me an even greater focus and determination to be who God has called me to be as a Believer. I am a son, brother, uncle, friend, McNeely Brothers Painting partner, U.S. Marine Vietnam Veteran, bus and prison ministry volunteer, Sunday School teacher, and Gideon. But most of all, I just want to be known as Big L: a man who loves and lives for God. I am a sinner that has been redeemed by the grace of God. He has changed my life, and I am sharing this book because I know, without a doubt, He can and will do the same for you. That, friends, is the heart of this book.

My prayer is that these inspirational poems will help you connect with God's truth in the middle of your need, and maybe even introduce you to the person of Jesus for the first time. I hope that they bless you like they blessed me as I wrote them.

In Christ,
Leonard McNeely

"Big L"

January 1

Luke 19:41-42

"As he approached Jerusalem and saw the city, he wept over it and said, if you, even you had only known on this day what would bring you peace, but now it is hidden from your eyes."

As Jesus rode down the street,
they threw cloaks at His feet.
They cheered and they sang,
because of the miracles they had seen.
When He saw the city, He did cry,
because the Messiah they failed to recognize.
Now instead of peace in their lives,
pain and suffering was their compromise.
When Jesus comes your way, don't say no- don't delay!
For His peace He wants you to have, this very day.

Jan. 2

Mark 15:2-5

"'Are you the king of the Jews?' asked Pilate. 'Yes, it is as you say.', Jesus replied. The chief priests accused him of many things. So Pilate asked him, 'Aren't you going to answer? See how many things they are accusing you of.' But Jesus still made no reply, and Pilate was amazed."

A kiss started it all,
the one who would give it all.
Pilate was the one he had to see,
to be killed or to be set free.
"Are you the king of the Jews"? Pilate asks that day.
Jesus replied, "It is as you say."
They accused Jesus of many things,
but no response would He bring.
So they released a criminal that was lost
and Jesus faced the cross.
For the hour had come,
that He would be hung,
bound by nails on a cross to die,
with the lost, in His eyes.

Jan. 3

Matthew 27:26

"Then He released Barabbas to them.
But he had Jesus flogged and handed
Him over to be crucified."

The decision was made to free Barabbas and take Jesus away,
To be flogged and crucified on that day.
When they drew back the whip with cat of nine tails,
Oh! The flesh flew, it was unreal.
A brutal beating He did receive,
and He did it for you and me.
What a price to pay, to set us free,
but that was God's plan, don't you see.

Jan, 4

Luke 23:27, 32-34

"A large number of people followed Him,
including women who mourned and wailed for Him.
Two other men both criminals, were also led out with Him
to be executed. When they came to the place called the skull.
There they crucified Him, along with the criminal's; one on His
right, the other on His left. Jesus said, 'Father forgive them for
they do not know what they are doing.'"

Weak and bleeding, Jesus and the others walked to the hill
Golgotha, where He would be killed.
His family and followers crying, thinking, "This can't be happening. This can't be real."
They drove the nails in His hands and feet,
shattering the bones as they went in deep.
With blood dripping to the ground,
Jesus lifted His head and looked around.
"Forgive them Father, for they do not know what they do".
With all He went through,
His heart and mind was on me and you.

Jan 5

Luke 23:42-43

"Then he said, 'Jesus, remember me when you come into your kingdom.' Jesus answered him, 'I tell you the truth, today you will be with me in paradise.'"

Two men hung beside Jesus that day.
The one on the left said, "Save us if you are who you say"- with no respect,
thinking of himself in his own way.
The one on the right had a change of heart,
he asked Jesus to remember him before his life would depart.
Now we are the ones on the right and left of the tree,
what will our decision be:
to ask Jesus to remember me?
or to depart from Jesus for all eternity?

Jan. 6

John 3:16

"For God so loved the world, that He gave His one and only Son, that whoever believes in Him shall not perish but have eternal life."

Three crosses on a hill,
the one in the middle, Love came to be fulfilled.
Soldiers on the ground
and people all around
women were crying, heartbroken, too,
as they watched Jesus suffer for me and you.
Angels were ready to come to his rescue,
but Jesus didn't give the cue,
He said, "This is what I came to do."
as He gave His life for me and you.

Jan 7

Luke 23:52-53

"Going to Pilate, he asked for Jesus body. Then he took it down,
wrapped it in linen cloth, and placed it in a tomb cut in the
rock, one in which no one had yet been laid."

Darkness came over all the land,
as Jesus cried, "It is finished!", and His spirit went into His
Father's hands.
Joseph wrapped the body real tight
with linens that were white.
In the tomb the body he did lay,
as the sin debt of mankind, was paid that day.

Jan 8

Luke 24:1-3, 6

"On the first day of the week, very early in the morning, the women took spices they had prepared and went to the tomb, they found the stone rolled away from the tomb, but when they entered they did not find the body of the Lord Jesus. He is not here, he has risen."

It was the first day of the week, early in the morning,
and just a few days earlier the women were mourning.
Now at the tomb with spices in hand,
they found no Jesus, but two men.
They said, "Why do you look for the living among the dead?
Jesus has risen just as He said".
Now go tell the eleven and all the others,
that Jesus is alive, my sisters, my brothers.

Jan. 9

Luke 24:36

"While they were still talking about this, Jesus himself
stood among them and said to them,
"Peace be with you."

The women, the eleven they did tell,
but doubt was in their heart, as on their ears, the good news fell.
Then Jesus appeared to them,
they were so startled and frightened, they were afraid of Him.
Then Jesus showed them his hands and feet,
and the doubt and fear from their hearts it did creep.
Repentance and forgiveness of sins will be preached in my name,
and you are the witnesses, the news to proclaim.
Wait and don't sigh,
you will be clothed with power from on high.

Jan 10

Luke 24:50-51

When he had led them out to the vicinity of Bethany. He lifted
up his hands and blessed them. While he was blessing them, He
left them and was taken up into heaven.

Jesus met with the disciples after His death,
on His command, fish filled their net.
He prepared breakfast for them to eat,
as they sat around on the beach.
The disciples were happy as they could be,
now Jesus, they could see.
He led them out, in the land.
He blessed them as He lifted His hands,
back to his father in heaven He would go,
back to the one that loves Him so.

Jan 11

Ephesians 1:7

"In Him we have redemption through his blood, the forgiveness
of sins, in accordance with the riches of God's grace."

In Jesus we have forgiveness of sin,
through the blood that ran down His chin.
As they pushed the crown of thorns on His head,
the blood poured. Oh! It was red.
His body covered in blood, racked with pain,
so we could be forgiven, is why He came.
It's only through His blood that we have redemption of our sins,
and the new life He gives will begin.

Jan, 12

Nahum 1:7

"The Lord is good, a refuge in times of trouble.
He cares for those who trust in Him."

When your troubles have you down
and you are wearing a frown,
go to God and say,
"Father will you help me today?"
He is always close by,
to answer your cry.

Jan. 13

Acts 16:30-31

"Sirs, what must I do to be saved? They replied,
'Believe in the Lord Jesus and you will be saved.'"

Broken, convicted of sin;
that's when salvation begins.
Believe and receive Jesus, and you will be saved,
and your sins will be washed away.

Jan 14

Acts 26:18

"To open their eyes, and to turn them from darkness to light,
and from the power of Satan to God so that they may receive
forgiveness of sins, and a place among those who are sanctified
by faith in me."

What the gospel will do,
if you let its light shine through:
It will relieve you from darkness that's all around,
and free you from Satan's power that has you bound.
It remits sins that are deep within,
and restores a lost inheritance with our friends.

Jan 15

Colossians 2:6-7

"So then, just as you received Christ Jesus as Lord, continue to live in Him, rooted and built up in Him, strengthened in the faith as you were taught, and overflowing with thankfulness."

Jesus we have received;
He is our Lord, our sufficiency.
In Him we will be strong,
and that's what will carry us on.
Oh, the blessings we will receive,
when our thankful hearts our Lord does see.

Jan 16

Proverbs 3:5-6

"Trust in the Lord with all your heart and lean not on your own understanding; in all your ways acknowledge Him, and He will make your paths straight."

Trust the Lord with your mind, spirit and soul.
He has to be the One in control.
For we don't know what is good for us,
so on Him we rely, on Him we trust.
And as we face each day,
He will help us, and show us the way.

Jan. 17

1 Peter 3:20b – 21

"...in the days of Noah while the Ark was being built. In it only a few people, eight in all were saved through water, and this water symbolizes baptism that now saves you also – not the removal of dirt from the body but the pledge of a good conscience toward God. It saves you by the resurrection of Jesus Christ."

The Ark was built for all to get on board,
but only eight were on when God shut the door.
The Ark is a picture of Jesus for us today:
He died for everyone so we could be saved.
Now we are the picture of the people of Noah's day,
we have the choice to except Jesus or go our own way.

Jan 18

Genesis 3:21

The Lord God made garments of skin for
Adam and his wife and clothed them.

John 3:36

Whoever believes in the son has eternal life, but whoever
rejects the son will not see life, for God's wrath remains on him.

God provided a covering for man's guilt and shame.
That's why death and shedding of blood had to be, that's
why He came.
He provided His son, the Lamb of God to cover our guilt and shame
and an opportunity to have eternal life, by believing on His
holy name.

Jan, 1 9

Psalm 86:5

"You are forgiving and good, O Lord,
abounding in love to all who call to you."

That old sin got you down?
Can't seem to get your head up from the ground?
The Lord is waiting for your call,
His love will catch you, no matter how far you fall.

Jan. 20

Colossians 3:5-6

"Put to death, therefore, whatever belongs to your earthly nature; sexual immorality, impurity, lust, evil desires and greed, which is idolatry. Because of these, the wrath of God is coming."

People think they can sin and do all kinds of wrong.
The heavens seem to be silent, so they carry on.
But the wrath of God is coming, and the heavens won't be silent any more,
people will have to pay the cost for the sin they bore.

Jan 21

Luke 12:29-31

"And do not set your heart on what you will eat or drink; do not worry about it. For the pagan world runs after all such things, and your Father knows that you need them. But, seek His kingdom, and these things will be given to you as well."

Father help me to trust even if I don't understand.
Help me to know everything is in your hands.
Help me to trust what You say,
and not all the noise that's in the world today.

Jan. 22

Philippians 2:5-8

"Let this mind be in you, which was also in Christ Jesus. Who,
being in the form of God, thought it not robbery to be equal
with God: but made himself of no reputation, and took upon
him the form of a servant, and was made in the likeness of men.
And being found in fashion as a man, humbled himself, and
became obedient unto death, even the death of the cross."

To obey and not rebel,
is what Jesus did, what he came to tell.
Let his mind be in you,
the one from heaven, who became human too.
He became a servant, in the likeness of men,
to help the poor, broken hearts to mend.
He humbled himself, and became obedient to death,
and you were on his mine, when he took his last breath.

Jan. 23

Luke 3:4, 6

"As is written in the book of the words of Isaiah the prophet:
A voice of one calling in the desert,
'Prepare the way for the Lord. . .
and all mankind will see God's salvation.'"

A Voice is calling today.
Its saying, "Repent, in your heart Jesus wants to stay."
Will we hear the voice and let Him in?
Jesus wants to save us, He wants to be our friend.

Jan. 24

Genesis 22:13-14

"Abraham looked up and there in a thicket he saw a ram caught
by its horns. He went over and took the ram and sacrificed it
as a burnt offering instead of his son. So Abraham called that
place the Lord will provide. And to this day it is said, 'On the
mountain of the Lord it will be provided.'"

The Lord will provide,
if you do not hide.
The Lord will provide,
if in Him you confide.
The Lord will provide all your needs;
it's about trust, and not the things we see.

Jan, 25

Genesis 2:15-17

"The Lord God took the man and put him in the Garden of Eden to work it and take care of it. And the Lord God command the man, 'You are free to eat from any tree in the garden, but you must not eat from the tree of the knowledge of good and evil, for when you eat of it you will surely die.'"

After God formed Adam from the ground, and made Eve from a rib,
He gave them a garden to work and to live.
They had fruit from the trees they were free to eat,
but from one, God said, "Do not eat".
Now in different forms, that fruit is still with us today,
and God tells us to stay away!

Jan. 26

Psalm 86:7

"In the day of my trouble, I will call to you,
for you will answer me."

Do you have trouble? Tell me- who don't!
But we don't have to go around all depressed and in want.
Because our Heavenly Father, out of His loving kindness and great care,
is eager to hear and answer our prayer.

Jan, 27

Hebrews 5:9

"And once made perfect, He became the source of eternal
salvation for all who obey Him."

Jesus was made perfect; this came to be,
when He stretched His arms across that tree.
He completed the work that had to be,
to save us from our sins, and set us free.
He has always been perfect, this is true,
but now He has perfected salvation for me and you.

Jan 28

Philippians 2:7

"Jesus took on the nature of a servant becoming a human
just like us."

If we act like Jesus, we won't demand what we think we deserve.
But we will be looking for ways that we can serve.

Jan 29

Genesis 15:3-5

"And Abram said, 'You have given me no children; so a servant
in my household will be my heir.' Then the word of the Lord
came to him, 'This man will not be your heir, but a son coming
from your own body will be your heir.' He took him outside
and said, 'Look up at the heavens and count the stars – if
indeed you can count them.' Then He said to him, 'so shall your
offspring be.'"

What we think will happen is not necessarily the way
things will be.
God has His plans, and they affect you and me.
He's our shield- do not be afraid.
Trust Him, for great rewards are on the way.

Jan. 30

Isaiah 54:10

"Though the mountains be shaken and the hills be removed, yet my unfailing love for you will not be shaken nor my covenant of peace be removed, says the Lord, who has compassion on you."

In our life we have ups and downs,
which bring smiles, which bring frowns.
At times we feel like our life is falling apart,
we lose courage, we lose heart.
We feel all alone, and that no one cares.
We forget, God's love and that He is always there.

Jan. 31

Genesis 1:26

"Then God said, 'Let us make man in our image, in our likeness,
and let them rule over the fish of the sea and the birds of the
air, over the livestock, over all the earth, and over all the creatures that move along the ground.'"

After God created the sun and the moon, the trees, animals, and
all there was in the land.
God said, "Let us make man."
Yes, that was His plan,
so we could be a part of His wonderful creation, made by is pow-
erful hand. Made like Him, with a spirit, body and soul;
for us to rule over the animal world was His goal.

Feb 1

Titus 3:5-6

"He saved us not because of righteous things we had done,
but because of his mercy. He saved us through the washing of
rebirth and renewal by the Holy Spirit, whom He poured out on
us generously through Jesus Christ our Savior."

When you were saved, you were washed.
"Oh my gosh", you say, "I don't remember being scrubbed
or rubbed".
It was not the normal washing you would think,
that you would take in a tub or a sink.
We were washed by the Holy Spirit, through Jesus - He
poured it out.
Now you remember because when that Spirit water hit you, you
could do nothing but shout!

Feb 2

Romans 4:20-21

"Yet he did not waver through unbelief regarding the promise
of God, but was strengthened in his faith and gave glory to
God, being fully persuaded that God had power to do what he
promised."

It's the most reasonable thing to do:
trust God's Word because it's true.
God's Word is the surest thing in the universe,
although some may want to converse.
You take no risk in believing it,
because God has the power to deliver it.

Feb. 3

Romans 1:17

"For in the gospel righteousness from God is revealed, a righteousness that is by faith from first to last, just as it is written:
the righteousness will live by faith."

We, who are not righteous, are treated as if we were,
that is clear in God's Word.
Jesus paid the penalty for our sins,
and our faith is where our righteousness begins.

Feb 4

Ephesians 5:13-14

"But everything exposed by the light becomes visible, for it is light that makes everything visible. This is why it is said: 'Wake up, o sleeper, rise from the dead, and Christ will shine on you.'"

Our ministry and witness is a light that others can see;
they are brought to the light through you and me.
Wicked men are transformed into children of light,
that's why we need to be close to Jesus,
so our light will be bright.

Feb 5

Titus 1:11-12

"For the grace of God that brings salvation has appeared to all men. It teaches us to say no to ungodliness and worldly passion, and to live self-controlled, upright and godly lives in this present age."

Let's not take it for granted,
God's grace appeared when the Lord Jesus visited our planet.
He appeared for the salvation of all men,
and His death and resurrection are sufficient for the redemption of all sin,
but it's so sad to say,
all won't answer His call before that day.

Feb 6

Romans 4:7-8

"Blessed are they whose transgressions are forgiven, whose sins are covered. Blessed is the man whose sin the Lord will never count against him."

No works does it take to be forgiven of our sins,
it's all through God's grace that forgiveness begins.
Our sins are covered by Jesus blood,
and the joy that fills our hearts is like a flood.
Oh! The sweet taste of forgiveness in this garden,
is experiencing God's full and complete pardon.

Feb 7

Philippians 2:5-7

"Your attitude should be the same as that of Christ Jesus, who, being in nature God, did not consider equality with God something to be grasped, but made Himself nothing, taking the very nature of a servant being made in human likeness."

Our attitude, how should it be?
Stuck on ourselves? It's all about me?
You could have an attitude like that,
but I don't think you want to wear that hat.
Thinking of others as better than ourselves is where we should be,
looking to Christ and what He has done for you and me.

Feb 8

Matthew 20:34

"Jesus had compassion on them and touched their eyes.
Immediately they received their sight
and followed Him."

To be blind is a bad place to be;
only the Lord can truly help you see.
When you finally can see and find your way,
close to Jesus, you want to stay.

Feb. 10

Ephesians 1:7

"In Him we have redemption through his blood, the forgiveness
of sins, in accordance with the riches of God's grace."

Oh! The power of His saving blood,
it keeps us from the wrath above.
When we called on Jesus name,
His blood covered our sin and our shame.
No judgment now will we see,
because of the blood Jesus shed on that tree.

Feb 11

Romans 14:21-22

"It is better not to eat meat or drink wine or do anything else
that will cause your brother to fall. So whatever you believe
about these things keep between yourself and God. Blessed is
the man who does not condemn himself by what he approves."

Could we be a log
that causes our brother to fall?
Or we that rock,
that their path we block?
We could be and not even know,
what we are doing causes them to stumble, and not to grow.
Be careful what we do in our brother's eyes,
we could cause hurt before we even realize.
So it's better to exercise your right,
with God out of sight.

Feb 12

Romans 10:11

"As the scripture says, 'Anyone who trusts in Him will never be put to shame.'"

To others we share Jesus' name,
and at first you may have feelings of shame.
But as you are sharing that wonderful name,
Jesus is doing the same
Sharing your name with God above,
that brought you salvation with all His love.

Feb 13

Proverbs 1:8-9

"Listen, my son, to your father's instruction and do not for sake your mother's teaching. They will be a garland to grace your head and a chain to adorn your neck."

By heeding to parental advice,
a young person can avoid a lot of stife.
Listen especially to your mothers
that love you like no other.
She loves you from the time she holds you on her knee,
even until you're six foot three.
Her godly advice will keep you strong,
which you need to carry on.
Moral beauty and honor in your life will be,
if you listen to the advice given from your mother's knee.

Feb 14

Romans 8:26-27

"In the same way, the spirit helps us in our weakness. We do not know what we ought to pray for, but the spirit himself intercedes for us with groans that words cannot express. And he who searches our heart knows the mind of the spirit because the spirit intercedes for the saints in accordance with God's will."

Just like we are encouraged by our hope of salvation,
we are also helped in our lack of communication.
Yes, our prayer life. See, we don't know how to pray,
so the Spirit prays what our heart really needs to say.
And because they are always in accordance with God's will, they
are for our good, no matter how we feel.

Feb 15

Romans 6:14

"For sin shall not be your master, because you are not under
law, but under grace."

The believer has died to sin,
and now the Holy Spirit lives within.
He's motivated by love for the Savior to do what's right,
and not by fear of punishment, like those who live in the night.
Yes, saved by grace, freed from the bondages of sin,
to serve the Lord, by the power of the Holy Spirit that lives within.

Feb-16

Romans 2:16

"This will take place on the day when God will judge men's
secrets through Jesus Christ, as my gospel declares."

No secrets will be kept on judgment day,
not a one will be hidden- they will all be put on display.
For all our secret sins in our life
will on that day come to light.
This is what the gospel proclaims,
and Jesus Christ is the Judge's name.

Feb, 17

Romans 1:12

"That is, that you and I may be mutually
encouraged by each other's faith."

What a blessing it is to meet with brothers and sisters in the Lord.
The love and encouragement they give is to be adored.
So when we meet, don't be shy,
share with someone as they walk by.
Shake a hand, hug one or two,
you will be encouraged before you are through.

Feb 18

Romans 10:9

"That if you confess with your mouth, Jesus is Lord, and believe
in your heart that God raised Him from the dead, you will
be saved."

If in your salvation you have a doubt,
confess with your mouth and let it out.
If salvation you want to be a part of,
then believe in the Lord from above.
Believe God raised Him from the dead,
you will be forgiven, with nothing to dread.

Feb 19

Romans 8:18

"I consider that our present sufferings are not worth comparing with the glory that will be revealed in us."

The pain and suffering we go through,
would seem small to me and you,
if we only knew the glory that awaits,
just beyond those pearly gates.

Feb 20

Romans 1:19-20

"Since what may be known about God is plain to them, because God has made it plain to them. For since the creation of the world God's invisible qualities, His eternal power and divine nature have been clearly seen, being understood from what has been made, so that men are without excuse."

Are those who never heard the gospel lost?
Will they experience God's wrath?
Will they suffer loss?
Well, this will make you scratch your head and cross your eyes; let's see where the answer lies.
As we look up into the sky, and see the sun, moon and stars shining bright,
God reveals Himself to all in sight.
Yes, God has revealed Himself to them in creation,
but they have not acknowledged this revelation.
To answer the question that has been turned loose:
They will be without excuse!

Feb. 21

John 3:17-18

"For God did not send His son into the world to condemn the world but to save the world through Him. Whoever believes in Him is not condemned, but whoever does not believe stands condemned already because he has not believed in the name of God's one and only son."

We are sinners and we will sin,
but we can go to Jesus, our Savior and our Friend.
He doesn't condemn- He forgives, and we have a new start, and
from His side we do not want to depart.

Feb 22

1 Peter 4:7-8

"The end of all things is near. Therefore be clear minded and self-controlled so that you can pray. Above all, love each other deeply, because love covers over a multitude of sins."

Here's some advice that will help us all,
for the end is near, when everything will fall.
Our prayer life should not be hindered by what's going on, for our fellowship with God will keep us strong.
We must work on our fellowship with members of the household of faith,
show them love and forgive them for their mistakes.

Feb, 23

James 2:26

"As the body without the spirit is dead, so faith without
deeds is dead."

Faith without works is what we are talking about today,
to trust God or go our own way.
The body without the spirit is lifeless- useless, you might say.
So faith without works is dead, in the same way.

Feb 24

Hebrews 10:22

"Let us draw near to God with a sincere heart in full assurance
of faith, having our hearts sprinkled to cleanse us from a guilty
conscience and having our bodies washed with pure water."

Just think, we can go to the God of all creation,
and in our hearts we have a grand celebration.
Oh! The peace, the joy we have,
it's like being on a cloud.
With a heart sincere,
we know our God is near;
His promises are for us,
in Him we can trust.
Washed by His blood our conscience is clear.
Oh! What a privilege! To God, we can draw near.

Feb 25

Hebrews 7:24-25

"But because Jesus lives forever, he has a permanent priest-hood. Therefore he is able to save completely those who come to God through him because he always lives to intercede for them."

There is no danger that any believers will be lost;
our eternal security rests on the cross.
His never ending intercession for us
is security we can trust.
He is able to save us for all time,
which from the beginning was God's mind.
Jesus is at God's right hand,
where death cannot interrupt God's plan.

Feb 26

Galatians 5:7-8

"You were running a good race. Who cut in on you and kept you from obeying the truth? That kind of persuasion does not come from the one who calls you."

To our Christian life, we had a good start,
Until something caused us to depart.
From the day we were saved, we trusted and obeyed.
But then confusion and doubt changed our way.
Pleasures, false teachings, and the world put our lives in a whirl.
They have taken us from the truth, from God's way, and that is where we are in our Christian life today.

Feb 27

1 Peter 1:23

"For you have been born again, not of perishable seed, but of imperishable, through the living and enduring word of God."

We are born by two kinds of seeds,
and you're saying, "What is he telling me?!"
The first seed is corruptible: human birth, subject to death and decay.
The second is different in every way:
incorruptible, born from the word of God, everlasting and with Him, we'll forever stay.

Feb 28

Job 11:13-18

"Put your heart right, Job. Reach out to God. Put away evil and wrong from your home. Then face the world again, firm and courageous. Then all your troubles will fade from your memory, like floods that are past and remembered no more. Your life will be brighter than sunshine at noon, and life's darkest hours will shine like the dawn. You will live secure and full of hope."

When tragedy you have been through,
all the crying and grief- you feel like you are about to come unglued.
You're numb and the pain you feel no more,
it's time to pick yourself up off the floor.
To face the future with courage, to move on,
with faith in God to make you strong.

Mar 1

Galatians 5:1

"It is for freedom that Christ has set us free. Stand firm,
then, and do not let yourselves be burdened again by a yoke
of slavery."

We have been set free from the slavery of sin,
by the blood that ran down Jesus' chin.
A cruel death on the cross,
was the price He paid for the lost.
Stand firm in this liberty,
for by grace we have been set free.

Mar 2

Galatians 1:11-12

"I want you to know, brothers that the gospel I preached is not something that man made up. I did not receive it from any man, nor was I taught it, rather I received it by revelation from Jesus Christ."

The gospel we hear today,
is not made up in anyway.
It wasn't taught to man,
it was received by revelation- that was God's plan.

Mar 3

James 4:13-16

"Now listen, you who say, today or tomorrow we will go to this or that City, spend a year there, carry on business and make money. Why, you do not even know what will happen tomorrow. What is your life? You are a mist that appears for a little while and then vanishes. Instead, you ought to say, if it is the Lord's will, we will live and do this or that. As it is, you boast and brag. All such boasting is evil."

We are always making plans: plans to do this or plans to go there, either by car or by air.
Plan your future if you dare,
but to leave God out is a scare.

Mar 4

Philippians 2:12-13

"Therefore, my dear friends, as you have always obeyed – not only in my presence but now much more in my absence – continue to work out your salvation with fear and trembling, for it is God who works in you to will and to act according to His good purpose."

We are to work out what God puts in;
this is obedience my dear friend.
As we read God's word, He shows us the way.
This keeps us close to Him and that's where we must stay, looking toward heaven all the way.

Mar 5

Hebrews 12: 26-27

"Once more I will shake not only the earth but also the heavens.
The words once more indicate the removing of what can be
shaken that is created things, so that what cannot be shaken
may remain."

There is coming a time and it won't be long
the heavens and earth will be gone.
This will be a command that comes from God's throne.
When all is destroyed and comes to an end,
God's kingdom will begin.
Only that which is real will remain,
those that were called by Jesus name.

Mar 6

Hebrews 8:12

"For I will forgive their wickedness and will remember their
sins no more."

God made a covenant with you and me,
it started on a hill hanging from a tree.
If we accept His son Jesus Christ,
He will forgive our sin and our bad ways,
and with Him forever we can stay.

·Mar 7

1 Corinthians 3:1-3

"Brothers, I could not address you as spiritual but as worldly
mere infants in Christ. I gave you milk, not solid food – you are
still worldly. For since there is jealousy and quarreling among
you, are you not worldly? Are you not acting like mere men?"

Milk is good, but if a baby stays on milk, it won't grow like
it should.
The same is true in the spiritual realm. On God's word we feed,
but for some, milk they need.
They hear God's Word, but do not apply,
in worldliness they want to lie.

Mar 8

Proverbs 16:3

"Commit to the Lord whatever you do,
and your plans will succeed."

As we live our lives, we have hopes and dreams and
at times we think they will never be seen.
To ensure that our dreams and goals will be achieved,
give them to God and believe.

Mar 9

2 Corinthians 1:9

"Indeed, in our hearts we felt the sentence of death. But this happened that we might not rely on ourselves but on God, who raises the dead."

The One who raised the dead is the only hope of man.
There is nothing we can do by our own hand.
Condemned and certainly doomed to die;
On ourselves we can't rely.
But truly trust the one on high.

Mar 10

1 Corinthians 3:12-13

"If any man builds on this foundation using gold, silver, costly stones, wood hay or straw, their work will be shown for what it is, because the Day will bring it to light. It will be revealed with fire, and the fire will test the quality of each person's work."

The foundation of Christ has been laid
and we are building on it each and every day.
Are we using gold, silver or costly stones,
which represent God's Word to make our building strong?
Or are we using wood, straw or hay,
which will make our building sway?
Which one will stand up to the fire that will test them one day?

Mar 11

Ephesians 2:1, 4-5

"As for you, you were dead in your transgressions and sins. But because of his great love for us, God who is rich in mercy, made us alive with Christ even when we were dead in transgressions, it is by grace you have been saved."

Lifeless toward God, dead in our trespasses and sins.
This is how it all started, this is how we begin.
But this is not how it has to end!
We can have life,
through Jesus Christ,
the One who gave His life
and paid the price,
so we all can have a brand new life.
That is so nice!

Mar 12

Romans 13:12

"The night is nearly over, the day is almost here. So let us put aside the deeds of darkness and put on the armor of light."

The world we live in,
is like a night of sin,
that's about to come to its end.
The day of eternal glory is about to dawn,
and as believers, to Christ we belong.
Any worldly clothes that we have on,
take off, so a holy life can be shown.

Mar 13

Romans 8:5

"Those who live according to the sinful nature have their minds set on what that nature desires, but those who live in accordance with the spirit have their minds set on what the spirit desires."

What is your mind set on?
Those things of the flesh, that we know are wrong?
This nature to God, does not be belong.
If your mind is set on God, and the things He desires,
this is the nature He requires.
What is your mind set on:
the flesh or the Throne?

mar 14

1 Corinthians 1:28-29

"He chose the lowly things of this world and the despised things, and the things that are not to nullify the things that are, so that no one may boast before him."

The people the world holds high in their eye,
God passes by.
But generally the one who is not considered great,
God considers to be first rate.
He loves to take up people for whom the world as no esteem.
These are the people God likes on His team.

7 Mar 15

Psalm 8:9

"O Lord, our Lord, how majestic is your name
in all the earth!"

As I stare into the sky
I see the moon, it's so bright, and it's so high.
And I hear the birds as they wake,
then I think of my Father who is so great.
As I take in the air I breathe,
and surrounded by all the beautiful trees.
With the heavens above my head,
my Father lives, He's not dead.
As the sun comes up and I see the dawn of a new day,
I know my Father's love, and with Him I will stay.

mar 16

Ephesians 3:19

"And to know this love that surpasses knowledge, that you may
be filled to the measure of all fullness of God."

The love of God is like an ocean without any shores,
it is impossible to fully explore.
But we can learn more about His love from day to day,
if we let His spirit show us the way.
And if we allow Jesus our cup to fill,
and we can know of His massive love, for it is real!

May 17

Ephesians 1:9-10

"And he made known to us the mystery of His will according to his good pleasure, which he purposed in Christ, to be put into effect when the times will have reached their fulfillment. To bring all things in heaven and earth together under one head, even Christ."

The mystery: Do you wonder what could it be?
Keep reading and you will see,
the secret God has revealed to you and me.
The millennium is the scene;
when Christ returns to earth is the theme.
The One who was rejected
will be accepted!
God's goal: to set up Christ as head over all things,
in heaven and earth. And do you know what this means?
Jesus Christ is the King!

Mar 18

Proverbs 21:3

"To do what is right and just is more acceptable to the Lord than sacrifice."

God is not interested in our ritual ways,
Obedience to his word is
Where he wants us to stay,

March 19

Psalm 119:105

"Your word is a lamp to my feet and a light for my path."

Life is like walking in the night-
You can't see what's in front, nor what's on the left or right.
But if you had a light so you could see your way,
in the dark, you wouldn't have to stray.

Mar 20

Romans 9:25

"As he says in Hosea: 'I will call them "my people" who are not my people; and I will call her "my loved one" who is not my loved one.'"

The mercy of God's hand,
to save sinful man.
We don't deserve His mercy or His love,
but He chose to prepare us for His glory above.

Mar 21

1 John 5:4

"For everyone born of God overcomes the world. This is the
victory that has overcome the world, even our faith."

How can we have victory over the world
That ole system that keeps us from God, and puts our life
in a whirl?
The one who is born again,
and on God they do depend:
on their faith they can rise above the world,
and their life won't be in the worldly whirl.

Mar 22

1 John 2:15-17

"Do not love the world or anything in the world. If anyone loves
the world, the love of the Father is not in him. For everything
in the world, the cravings of sinful man, the lust of his eyes
and the boasting of what he has and does- come not from the
Father but from the world. The world and its desire pass away,
but the man who does the will of God lives forever."

The worldly system, we should not get involved in,
it will keep us from our Father, our friend.
It is a system that man has made,
away from Christ is His way.
The world and its desires pass away,
but the One who trusts God, forever will he stay.

Mar 23

1 John 1:5-7

"God is light in Him is no darkness at all. If we claim to have fellowship with him yet walk in the darkness, we lie and do not live by the truth. But if we walk in the light as he is in the light, we have fellowship with one another, and the blood of Jesus, His son, purifies us from all sin."

Now fellowship with God has some requirements for you and me, its plain to see!
Since God is light and in Him is no darkness at all,
there can't be any hidden sin, or our fellowship will hit a brick wall.
But if we walk in the light, our fellowship with Him will be oh so right!
For the blood of Jesus cleans us from all sin,
and our walk with darkness comes to an end.

Mar 24

Philippians 4:6-7

"Do not be anxious about anything but in everything, by prayer
and petition, with thanksgiving. Present your request to God
and the peace of God, which transcends all understanding, will
guard your hearts and your mind in Christ Jesus."

Worry can lead us to despair,
and we end up pulling our hair.
There's another way, but it takes trust,
and leaving worry behind is a must.
Worry and trust cannot be,
it has to be one or the other, don't you see!
Trust God with everything great or small,
and the peace which falls will run ole worry away, once and for all.

Mar 25

1 John 1:3-4

"We proclaim to you what we have seen and heard, so that you also may have fellowship with us. And our fellowship is with the Father and with his son Jesus Christ, we write this to make our joy complete."

Our fellowship with one another
comes from Jesus, my dear brothers.
Fellowship with God the Father, and son Jesus Christ,
makes our fellowship oh so nice.
It is a wonderful thing to have fellowship with the King,
and realize the forgiveness that He brings.
No earthly circumstance can take this joy away,
for it is in our hearts and there it will stay.

Mar 26

Matthew 4:10

"Jesus said to him, 'Away from me Satan! For it is written:
Worship the Lord your God, and serve him only.'"

Temptations can be hard for us,
especially those that draw us because of our own lust.
When Jesus was tempted by Satan, it wasn't a breeze;
He struggled like you and me.
But when He used His Father's word,
Satan had to flee like a bird.
For our worship Satan longs,
but our worship and service belong to God alone.

Mar 27

Matthew 15:8-9

"These people honor me with their lips, but their hearts are far
from me. They worship me in vain, their teachings are but rules
taught my men."

Do we say one thing and then another?
Do we take care of our father and mother?
Do we say one thing and then another?
Or do we help others. . .do we help our brother?
To honor God just with our lips, He will have no part.
Our worship to Him, must come from the heart.

Mar 28

1 John 3:16-18

"This is how we know what love is: Jesus Christ laid down his
life for us, and we ought to lay down our lives for our brothers.
If anyone has material possessions and sees his brother in need
but has no pity on him, how can the love of God be in him? Dear
children, let us not love with words or tongue but with actions
and in truth."

Love is good for you and me,
for Jesus gave it to us on the cross of Calvary.
Now, will we keep it for ourselves?
Or share it with someone else?
Will we help someone in need?
Or keep this love just for you and me?
In thinking about what to do,
remember what Christ did for you.

Mar 29

1 John 2:1-2

"My dear children, I write this to you so that you will not sin.
But if anybody does sin, we have one who speaks to the Father
in our defense – Jesus Christ, the righteousness one. He is the
atoning sacrifice for our sins, and not only for ours but also for
the sins of the whole world."

He is still our Father even if we sin,
Our fellowship will not end,
our relationship will not bend.
Sin should not be,
but we have One that defends you and me,
for He took all our sins on Calvary.

Mar 30

Isaiah 26:3-4

"You will keep in perfect peace him whose mind is steadfast,
because he trusts in you. Trust in the Lord forever, for the Lord,
the Lord, is the rock eternal."

Is there peace in your life to be found?
Are you discouraged - your heart wearing a frown?
Well lift your weary head,
lean on Jesus instead.
He will give you perfect peace,
the kind that will not cease.
Trust in Jesus, He's the rock that won't let you down.
And you won't have to wear that frown

mar. 31

Ephesians 6:8

"And pray in the spirit on all occasions, with all kinds of prayers
and requests. With this in mind, be alert and always keep on
praying for all the saints."

What an awesome thing,
to be able to talk to God through Jesus' name.
The One who created heaven and earth,
the One who gave us second birth.
The One who forgives our sins,
and never remembers them again.
To know He cares and feel His love,
as it comes from heaven above.
Oh, the sweetness of the time,
spent with the One, holy and divine.

April 1

Colossians 1:15

"He is the image of the invisible God,
the firstborn over all creation."

Image is something we can see,
but God is invisible to you and me.
He is a spirit, don't you see.
Then how is it He can be seen?
Well, in the person of Jesus Christ, don't you realize,
God made Himself visible to our mortal eyes.

April 2

1 John 3:2

"Dear friends, now we are children of God, and what we will be has not yet been made known. But we know that when he appears, we shall be like him."

Here in life, as we put our faith in God's word,
we know it's from Him we have heard.
The process of becoming like Christ is going on,
and it will continue until we go home.
We will be complete when we see Him,
standing in that heavenly realm.

April 3

Isaiah 40:29

"He gives strength to the weary
and increase the power of the weak."

Are you discouraged and wondering if God still cares for you,
The One who has always provided, the One who's seen
you through?
What kind of thinking is that?! Do you think He cares less for you
than He does the animals and the birds?
How absurd!
Strength will come to those who trust and wait;
that you don't have to debate.

april 4

Matthew 1:22-23

"All this took place to fulfill what the Lord had said through the prophet. 'The virgin will be with child and give birth to a son, and they will call Him Immanuel, which means God with us.'"

It all happened through a virgin birth
that God said would come, and be with us on earth.
Oh, the miracle of it all, as we think, as we recall.
God provided a savior for us all.

Note: Isaiah 7:14
This was told 700 years before Christ.

April 5

Romans 3:22-24

"This righteousness from God comes through faith in Jesus
Christ to all who believe. There is no difference for all have
sinned and fall short of the glory of God. And are justified freely
by his grace through the redemption that came by Christ Jesus."

Righteousness is from God, through faith in Jesus Christ,
don't you see!
It's for all who will believe and receive.
Yes, sinners like you and me,
by His grace can be set free.

april 6

Ephesians 1:3

"Praise be to the God and Father of our Lord Jesus Christ, who
has blessed us in the heavenly realms with every spiritual
blessing in Christ."

All who know God bless His Holy name,
for joy to his heart, praises do bring.
We bless Him by praising Him and giving Him all our love.
He blesses us and makes us glad by showering us with His blessings from above.

april 7

Isaiah 26:3

"You will keep in perfect peace him whose mind is steadfast,
because He trusts in you."

Where is our mind, where is our thoughts on
our problems or on our faults?
Jesus will keep us in perfect peace,
if on Him we trust, and Him we seek.

April 8

Romans 8:14

"For as many as are led by the spirit of God,
they are the sons of God."

We are the sons of God, you and me.
When we believed on Jesus, He set us free.
By His spirit we are led,
Nothing to fear, nothing to dread.
Worship means we are a part of God's family,
and we have to take up our responsibility:
to walk close to Him, and share His great love
that only comes from God above.

April 9

Romans 6:12-13

"Do not let sin control the way you live, do not give in to its lustful desires, instead, give yourselves completely to God since you have been given new life."

Have a battle within?
Good trying to win over sin.
You want to do what's right,
but old sin causes a fight.
Who can free me of this sin?
The answer is Jesus, my friend.
His blood covers our sin.
Now to him we must go,
for our sin to be controlled.
The more on his word you feed,
the less sin will have a hold on you and me.

april /0

Psalm 55:22

"Cast your cares on the Lord and he will sustain you,
he will never let the righteous fall."

When our hearts are filled with anguish, fear and trembling on
our hearts do fall,
and we can't get away from it all.
There's one thing we can do,
cry out to Jesus, who cares for me and you.
He bore the burden of our sins,
and through Him we have life that never ends.
And now He will bear our burdens and cares
if only to Him, we will share.

April 11

John 1:1,9

"In the beginning was the word, and the word was with God
and the word was God. The true light that gives light to every
man was coming into the world."

Jesus was God right from the start,
Jesus and God the same, but apart.
He had no beginning, but existed from all eternity,
His purpose is to bring light to humanity.

April 12

Proverbs 18:24

"A man that hath friends must show himself friendly: and there
is a friend that sticketh closer than a brother."

Friendliness wins friends,
are they for real or just pretend.
There will be some that will be with you through thick and thin,
and some will leave you like a leaf blown by the wind.
There is One, the Name above all names,
He never changes, and He stays the same.
Stay close to Him; for He's a winner,
He is a friend to all sinners.

April 13

Psalm 31:24

"Be of good courage, and he shall strengthen your heart,
all ye that hope in the Lord."

When you feel like there is no hope,
and you are at the end of your rope.
Be courageous; be strong,
for your hope in God is never wrong.

April 14

Psalm 91:1-2

"He who dwells in the shelter of the most high will rest in the shadow of the almighty. I will say of the Lord, he is my refuge and my fortress, my God, in whom I trust."

Jesus: in God, He did trust.
What does that say to the rest of us?
Unbroken fellowship with His Father, don't you see,
He never did anything with which His Father didn't agree.
He was perfectly God, perfectly man,
He lived His life in complete dependence on His Father in this land.
At any time and any day,
He could look up to His Father and say:
"My refuge and my fortress, my God, in him I trust."
Now, what does that say to the rest of us?

April 15

Isaiah 1:18-20

"'Come now, let us reason together", says the Lord. 'Though your sins are like scarlet, they shall be as white as snow; though they are red as crimson, they shall be like wool. If you are willing and obedient, you will eat the best from the land, but if you resist and rebel, you will be devoured by the sword.' For the mouth of the Lord has spoken."

Rebellion can lead to a life of shame,
but that can be changed if we call on Jesus's name.
"Come now, let us reason together", says the Lord;
He's wanting us to get on board.
No effort on our part can bring about change,
it only comes by believing on His holy name.
If we believe,
blessings we receive,
but destruction awaits those who rebel,
it's clear as a bell.

April 16

1 Peter 3:10-12

"For, whoever would love life and see good days must keep his tongue from evil and his lips from deceitful speech. He must turn from evil and do good, he must seek peace and pursue it. For the eyes of the Lord are on the righteous and his ears are attentive to their prayer, but the face of the Lord is against those who do evil."

"Enjoy life to the hilt! Experience good days!"
That all sounds good- show me the way!
Refrain from speaking evil or deceit,
if you want the good life to be complete.
Not only evil speech, but evil deeds are not to be.
Repay evil with good and promote peace,
and the Lord's blessings will not cease.

April 17

Matthew 12:50

"For whoever does the will of my Father in heaven is my
brother and sister and mother."

We are brothers to the King. Really! Can this be?
Yes, Jesus included us in His plan of salvation,
don't you see.
It all happened when His own people wouldn't believe.
Whoever does His Father's will, becomes His brother-
that's for real!

April 19

John 16:23-24

"In that day you will no longer ask me anything. I tell you the truth, my Father will give you whatever you ask in my name. Until now you have not asked for anything in my name. Ask and you will receive, and joy will be complete."

Father we pray in Jesus name,
knowing You are different, but the same.
When we pray in Jesus name,
it's His holiness and righteousness, we do claim.
When we ask, we will receive,
because it's in Jesus we believe.
Joyful our hearts will be,
when answers to our prayers, we do receive.

apri 20

John 6:35

"Then Jesus declared, I am the bread of life. He who comes to me will never go hungry, and he who believes in me will never be thirsty."

Come to Jesus and you will see
He will satisfy your spiritual needs.
No more emptiness in your life will be,
when you fill up with the One who gave His life for you and me.

April 21

Luke 2: 13-14

"Suddenly, a great company of the heavenly host appeared with the angel, praising God and saying, 'Glory to God in the highest, and on earth, peace to men on whom His favor rest.' "

Real peace comes when in Jesus we receive,
a lasting peace for you and me.
A peace of mind and of soul,
with all the many blessings untold.
Yes we find favor with God through Jesus who took our sins,
so we could have peace with God that never ends.

April 22

Isaiah 40:31

"But they that wait upon the Lord shall renew their strength;
they shall mount up with wings as eagles; they shall run, and
not be weary, and they shall walk and not faint."

Feeling weary and beat down,
from all the sin that does abound.
Everywhere wrong is winning over right,
and you feel helpless in the fight.
Lift up your head to the one on high,
He'll give you new strength, you'll feel like you could fly.
He will lift up your weak weary bones,
and in the fight we can carry on.

April 23

Romans 4:20-21

"Yet he did not waver through unbelief regarding the promise of God, but was strengthened in his faith and gave glory to God, being fully persuaded that God had power to do what he promised."

To trust God is the best thing we can do,
for He won't lie to me and you.
Honoring Him as One who can be depended on,
for His promises are never wrong.
He is fully able to carry them through,
and we take no risk in believing they are true.

April 24

1 Corinthians 14:33

"For God is not a God of disorder, but of peace."

The Holy Spirit lives in you and me,
but is He in control? How can we see?
If a meeting is the scene of screaming and yelling, and name telling out of your lips do roll,
you can be sure that the spirit of God is not in control.

April 25

2 Corinthians 5:21

"God made Him who had no sin to be sin for us, so that in Him
we might become the righteousness of God."

Thank you Jesus for dealing with the whole problem of sin.
Through You alone, life begins.
Now in God's sight we are made right,
for Your blood hides our sin from His sight.

april 26

Proverbs 15:1-2

"A gentle answer turns away wrath, but a harsh word stirs up anger. The tongue of the wise commends knowledge, but the mouth of the fool gushes folly."

Have you ever been in a shouting spat?
Harsh words are used: "You are this!" and,
"You are that!"
Wonder what a different conversation it would be,
if instead you answered back calmly?
The tongue is very hard to rule,
but if you tame it, you won't be like the fool.

April 27

John 1:12-13

"Yet to all who received him, to those who believed in his name,
he gave the right to become children of God. Children born not
of natural decent, nor of human decision or a husband's will,
but born of God."

God's children - how can we be?
It's not from good works or from the family seed.
No, we have to receive and believe in His name,
then we will be His, forever changed.

April 28

1 Corinthians 1:8-9

"He will keep you strong to the end, so that you will be
blameless on the day of our Lord Jesus Christ. God, who has
called you into fellowship with his son, Jesus Christ our Lord, is
faithful."

As we wait for Christ's return,
He will keep us strong- that is confirmed.
This is because of what Christ has done,
and not what we, in our life have begun.
Because we have trusted Christ,
God keeps us- isn't that nice!
We have been called into the fellowship with His Son.
He will forever be the Faithful One.

april 29

Joel 2:26

"And ye shall eat in plenty, and be satisfied, and praise the name of the Lord your God, that hath dealt wondrously with you: and my people shall never be ashamed."

God takes care of His children, that you can believe.
His eye is forever on you and me.
Praise His great name,
and never be ashamed
of our wonderful God, that will never change.

april 30

Psalm 63:1

"O God, you are my God, earnestly I seek you; my soul
thirst for you, my body longs for you, in a dry
and weary land where there is no water."

A relationship we have you and me,
I trust and depend on you to meet my need.
I look for you when all goes wrong,
For in your strength I am strong.
You are my God and in you I will dwell,
For I know your love will never fail

May 1

Matthew 5:6

"Blessed are those who hunger and
thirst for righteousness, for they will be filled."

To hunger and thirst,
we think of our stomach first.
But to hunger and thirst after righteousness, there will be peace;
there will be rest,
as we draw near our Lord, who knows us best.
He will satisfy our hungry soul,
and then our hearts will be warm and not stone cold.
So, belly up to His word today,
and you will be filled before you go away.

May 2

Psalm 145:15-16

"Cast not away therefore your confidence, which hath great recompence of reward. The eyes of all wait upon thee; and thou givest them their meat in due season. Thou openest thine hand, and satisfies the desire of every living thing."

Do not lose trust
in the one that provides for us.
His provisions, they are great!
They are worth the wait.
All creatures look to Him,
for their food to be provided to them.
With no greater effort than opening His hand,
He feeds his numberless creatures throughout the land.

May, 3

2 Timothy 3:16-17

"All scripture is God breathed and is useful for teaching, rebuking, correcting and training in righteousness, so that the man of God maybe thoroughly equipped for every good work."

The scriptures are God breathed- it was written for you and me.
The Bible gives spiritual nourishment as we read,
it fulfills our every need.
It shows us where we're wrong,
and reading regularly, it will make us strong.
It teaches us to live godly lives,
and equips for the work, that before us lies.

May 4

Matthew 6:24

"No one can serve two masters.
Either he will hate the one and love the other, or he will be
devoted to the one and despise the other.
You cannot serve both God and money."

God or money which will it be?
They present rival claims, don't you see.
A choice must be made by you and me,
God or materialism: which will it be?
Will we live for temporal things,
and the short time joy that it brings?
Or follow Jesus with everlasting joy and peace,
and enjoy a life that will not cease?

May 5

1 Corinthians 2:9

"No eye has seen, no ear has heard, no mind has conceived
what God has prepared for those who love him."

In our human wisdom, we cannot see
the spiritual blessings God has for you and me.
The ear receives,
but can't perceive,
the mind can't comprehend
or even begin to understand
what God has for man.
Only through the spirits power,
we will know what's truly ours.

May 6

Hebrews 12:2-3

"Let us fix our eyes on Jesus the author and perfecter of our faith, who for the joy set before him endured the cross, scorning its shame, and sat down at the right hand of the throne of God. Consider him who endured such opposition from sinful men, so that you will not grow weary and lose heart."

How do we continue to walk with God each and every day,
and face the struggles that come our way?
There is only one way that will help us through,
keeping our eyes on Jesus, that went to the cross for me and you.
He set His eyes on the joy He would gain,
this helped Him through the suffering and shame the cross did bring.
Now He's beside God on His throne,
no more shame or suffering to Him belong.

May 7

Hebrews 2:14

"Since the children have flesh and blood, He too, shared in their humanity so that by His death He might destroy him who holds the power of death. That is the devil."

Satan is roaming around,
opposing God's work, being confound.
His time is short, don't you see.
His doom is a guarantee.
He received a death wound at the cross,
he knows his time is short: he has lost.

May 8

Psalm 100:1-4

"Shout for joy to the Lord all the earth. Worship the Lord with
gladness, come before him with joyful songs. Know that the
Lord is God, it is he who made us and we are his, we are his
people the sheep of his pasture. Enter his gates with thanksgiving and his courts with praise, give thanks to him and praise
his name."

Shout for Joy!
For we have our salvation to enjoy.
We have freedom from the bondage of sin,
on our face should be a great big grin.
Serving our Lord with gladness
and not sadness;
coming before Him with praise,
our voices we do raise.
Singing to our King,
the One to whom we cling.
Be thankful to Him and bless His name,
for it's His love we do claim.

May. 9

Deuteronomy 13:4

"Ye shall walk after the Lord your God, and fear him, and keep His commandments, and obey His voice, and ye shall serve Him, and cleave unto him."

For God, our life we shall live.
Believe His work, and know He's real.
Listening to His small still voice,
knowing in our heart, He's our choice.
Staying close to Him, and sharing His name,
our lives will never be the same.

May 10

Ephesians 1:13-14

"And you also were included in Christ when you heard the
word of truth, the gospel of your salvation. Having believed,
you were marked in him with a seal, the promised Holy Spirit
our inheritance until the redemption of those who are God's
possession – to the praise of his glory."

How can we be sure that we will get God's inheritance some day?
Is it by how we live or what we say?
NO!
The Holy Spirit is our guarantee,
He seals you and me.
Our inheritance is safe and secure,
that we can be sure.

May 11

Ephesians 6:12

"For our struggle is not against flesh and blood, but against the rulers, against the authorities, against the powers of this dark world and against the spiritual forces of evil in the heavenly realms."

Old Satan, he is crafty as can be,
he wants us to think the trouble we see is caused by you and me.
And this may be true, to a certain extent,
but its Satan and his demons causing all the discontent.
He causes us to hate one another
He doesn't want us to love our brother.
This doesn't have to be because our strength is in the Lord, and his might.
Through Jesus, Satan we can fight.

May. 12

John 14:21

"Whoever has my commands and obeys them, he is the one
who loves me. He who loves me will be loved by my Father, and
I, too, will love him and show myself to him."

Our love for God, how is it known?
Is it a quick prayer, then we're gone?
To read a verse or two then we're through,
and it's off to another day for me and you.
Now these things are good, and they are right;
what we have to do is apply them to our life.
Yes, obey what God tells us to do,
this way we will know our love is true
and we will see God working through me and you.

May 13

Romans 12:10, 11, 13

"Be kindly affectioned one to another with brotherly love, in honor preferring one another. Not slothful in business, fervent in spirit, serving the Lord. . .distributing to the necessity of saints given to hospitality."

Brotherly love, yes, it should be
devoted to one another, through Christ our King.
Honor one another above yourselves
and never leave zeal on the shelf.
Serving the Lord with intense passion,
with joy and hope, we should fashion.
We will have afflictions too,
where we can faithfully pray each other through.
And for those in need,
we can practice our hospitality.

May 14

Romans 5:1-2

"Therefore, since we have been justified through faith,
we have peace with God through our Lord Jesus Christ,
through whom we have gained access by faith into
this grace in which we now stand. And we rejoice
in the hope of the glory of God."

We are made right in His sight,
through faith in the Son, who sits on His right.
No more guilt for what we have done,
for we are freed by the Son.
Now we are complete, we are whole,
as we experience the peace that floods our soul.
Now, into his grace we can stand,
because Jesus stretched out his hands.

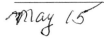

May 15

Romans 8:16-17

"The spirit himself testifies with our spirit that we are God's
children. Now if we are children, then we are heirs-heirs of God
and co-heirs with Christ, if indeed we share in his sufferings in
order that we may also share in his glory."

We are God's children, so the spirit does testify,
which brings us privileges from the One on high.
Heirs, if you will, of God above,
that through Jesus, shared His great love.
Although we may suffer for the name of Christ,
to live for Him, would be good advice.
In glory it will be,
we will share in our Father's wealth, as far as the eye can see.

May 16

Isaiah 64:8

"Yet, O Lord, you are our Father, we are the clay, you are the potter, we are all the work of your hand."

You can be grumpy, you can be sad
Or you can have a heart that's always glad.
It's our choice don't you see,
A grumpy heart- it doesn't have to be.
We have problems each and every day,
But a worried, sad heart won't make them go away.
If we trust Jesus, don't you see,
We will have a heart that's worry free.
God sees our hearts today.
Are we trusting Him or going our own way?

May 17

1 John 5:11

"And this is the testimony. God has given us
eternal life, and this life is in his son."

Eternal life God has given us,
if in His son Jesus, we do trust.
If you have Jesus in your heart,
eternal life will not part.
Eternal life will not be,
if Jesus is not in your heart, don't you see.
Eternity is for all who believe
that Jesus is God's son, and He died for you and me.

May 18

Jeremiah 7:23

"But I gave them this command:
Obey me, and I will be your God and you will be my people.
Walk in all the ways I command you,
that it may go well with you."

God we should obey,
and close to Him we should stay.
To stray away and not listen to His commands
would be a bad plan.
If our lives are to be well,
in Him we should dwell.

May 19

Psalm 63:3-5

"Because thy loving kindness is better than life, my lips shall praise thee. Thus will I bless thee while I live: I will lift up my hands in thy name. My soul shall be satisfied as with marrow and fatness, and my mouth shall praise thee with joyful lips."

With joyful lips I will speak,
of the God that I seek.
The God of mercy, the God of love,
that sent His son Jesus from above.
To hell, I will not go,
for on the cross, His love He did show.
He took my sins, and now I'm clean,
now on him I do lean.
When this life is over, with Him I'll stay,
because of His love on that day.

May 20

Romans 8:10

"But if Christ is in you, your body is dead because of sin,
yet your spirit is alive because of righteousness."

Before sin,
we had life that would never end.
The lion laid down with the lamb, and there was beauty
all around.
The food was in abundance, plenty to be found.
Fellowship with God, man had,
he was happy not sad.
Then sin entered in
and fellowship with God came to an end.
Death came to all,
as man had a great fall.
In God's great mercy and love,
He sent Jesus from above.
On the cross Jesus did hang,
to restore our fellowship with God, is why He came.

May 21

Philippians 2:9-11

"Therefore God exalted him to the highest place and gave him
the name that is above every name.
That at the name of Jesus every knee shall bow, in heaven and
on earth and under the earth, and that every tongue confess
that Jesus Christ is Lord."

Jesus is Lord, yes indeed;
at the sound of His name everything bows a knee.
God lifted Him up high;
His name is above the sky.
He came to earth, His purpose, to die.
Yes, every knee will bow and every tongue will confess
that Jesus is Lord. That, no one can contest.

May 22

1 John 4:13-16

"We know that we live in him and he in us, because he has given us of his spirit. And we have seen and testify that the father has sent his son to be the savior of the world. If anyone acknowledges that Jesus is the Son of God, God lives in him and he in God. And so we know and rely on the love God has for us."

Are there times when you feel you're not loved,
or been taken advantage of?
Being important is not real,
because of how the people around you make you feel.
Think on this! You are valuable- and important too!
Why else would God send his Son to die for you?
Yes, you are worthy, and loved too,
by a God that wants to spend eternity with you.
So lift your head, and don't you cry,
you are a child of the One on high.

May 23

1 John 4:9-10

"This is how God showed His love among us: He sent His one
and only Son into the world that we might live through him.
This is love, not that we loved God, but that he loved us and
sent His son as an atoning sacrifice for our sins."

Who can understand so great of a love,
that God would send His only Son from above.
To die on a cruel cross,
for those who are lost.
This is how God showed His love to us,
so in Jesus we could trust.
Yes, through Jesus we have eternal life.
He was the ultimate sacrifice.

May 24

John 6:47

"Verify, verify, I say unto you he that believeth on me hath everlasting life."

It's not the work we do or keeping the law.
This doesn't have anything to do with it at all
It's not our church membership or
Keeping the golden rule, that will give this
life to me and you.
But simply by believing in the Lord Jesus Christ,
the one that went to the cross and gave his life

May 25

Romans 8:29

"For those God foreknew He also predestined
to be conformed to the likeness of His Son.
That He might be the firstborn among many brothers."

God's character we are to become,
more and more like Jesus, His Son.
To be filled with love and kindness, too.
Then, joy and happiness will follow you.
Get rid of those sins that slow you down that
keep us wrapped up, that keep us bound.
Spend time with Jesus every day
and the sin that has you shackled will go away.
When life gets hard and life gets rough,
remember the reward that waits for us.

May 27

Mark 7:20-23

"What comes out of a man is what makes him unclean. For from within, out of mens hearts, come evil thoughts, sexual immorality, theft, murder, adultery, greed, malice, deceit, lewdness, envy, slander, arrogance and folly. All these evils come from inside and makes a man unclean."

What we eat, does that make us unclean?
Is that why some people are so mean?
What enters a man from the outside
Is that where our thoughts arrive?
Could it be that what enters a man from the outside is what makes him unclean?
I don't think that is what it means.
An impure heart
is where it all starts.
Yes, what comes out from within,
that causes us to sin.

May 28

Psalm 60:12

"With God we will gain the victory,
and he will trample down our enemies."

A victorious life you think we could achieve,
by being successful in all that we seek.
We put hope in our own desires and plans,
but victory doesn't come until we put it all in Jesus hands.
Success comes from our problems, failures, and weaknesses, you see,
as we trust in Jesus, on bended knee.
Depending on Jesus, it's clear to see,
is the only way we can truly succeed.
Problems, failures, weakness? Don't hang your head!
Look at Jesus, our Lord and Savior, instead.
Real victory comes from the blood He shed.

May 29

Exodus 13:18

"So God led the people around by the desert road toward the Red Sea. The Israelites went up out of Egypt ready for battle."

Also read Exodus 13:17-22, 14:1-18

The Israelites felt hopeless, we may too.
But there is hope in Jesus to pull us through.
The short way is not always best.
We have to trust God and His word in this test.
God may take us the long way around,
but he never lets us down.
He leads us when we cannot see,
to bring glory to Himself. Let it be.
Trust Him, praise Him, for what He has done for you and me.
For His love He showed as He hung on that tree.

May 30

1 Thessalonians 5:18

"Give thanks in all circumstance, for this is God's
will for you in Christ Jesus."

Complain or be thankful: which do I choose?
I will be thankful, for that way I can't lose.
A thankful heart has plenty room for the Lord,
Your load will be lighter, you can soar.
The One that blesses us and keep us all close-
He provides all our needs, so we can't boast.
Choose to be thankful and He will draw near.
Even His voice you can hear.
So be thankful today and you will see,
a different person you can be.

June 1

Luke 2:8-11

"And there were shepherds living out in the fields nearby, keeping watch over their flocks at night. An angel of the Lord appeared to them, and the glory of the Lord shone around them, and they were terrified. But he angel said to them, 'Do not be afraid, I bring you good news of great joy that will be for all the people. Today in the town of David a Savior has been born to you, He is Christ the Lord.'"

We love to hear good news, it warms our heart, and puts a smile on our face,
and sometimes we get so excited, that our heart wants to race.
Good news, what a joy it brings to our life, gets us away from all the strife.
Good news brings hope to our souls, its news that consoles.

June 2

Philippians 4:7

"And the peace of God, which transcends all understanding, will
guard your hearts and your minds in Christ Jesus."

It seems our problems are bigger than life itself,
And at times, we feel hopeless without any help.
But if we will look to our Father, full of love,
He will take our problems and stress, and we can watch them fly
away like a dove.
We will always have problems, that's guaranteed.
But our Father says, "Stay close to me.
For you are weak and I am strong.
I will carry you all day long."

June 3

Romans 15:13

"May the God of hope fill you with all joy and peace
as you trust in Him, so that you may overflow
with hope by the power of the Holy Spirit."

When you are weak and have no hope,
grab hold of Jesus's rope.
He will pull you up out of that miry clay
of depression and self-pity that drags you down all day.
The more you cling to this wonderful cord,
the stronger you will be in the Lord.
So grab a hold and hang on tight,
and you will see His marvelous light.

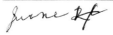

Matthew 11:28-30

"Come to me, all you who are weary and burdened, and I will give you rest. Take my yoke upon you and learn from me, for I am gentle and humble in heart and you will find rest for your souls. For my yoke is easy and my burden is light."

What will I fill my heart with today:
Fear or peace? What will I say?
If I allow my heart to be filled with fear,
Then I am not trusting Jesus, the One who's always near.
When I worry about my problems and what is to be,
That is when fear will have a hold on me.
If I trust Jesus, all fear has to flee,
And His rest and peace I will receive.
It is peace in my heart I want today,
As I rest in Jesus, my fear and anxiety go away.

June 5

Romans 8:16

"The Spirit himself testifies with our spirit that
we are God's children."

God's children. This is what we are called.
How does this happen? Any idea at all?
We come to God full of rebellion and mistakes,
Yet He is full of justice, so our sin we can't erase.
But because of His love, He wants to know us face to face.
So what did He do?
He punishes Himself on the cross for me and you.
So justice and love prevail
To keep us out of hell.
We are forgiven and our sins are washed away,
By the blood He shed on the cross that day.

June 6

Proverbs 22:17 & 19

"Pay attention and listen to the sayings of the wise,
apply your heart to what I teach...
So that your trust may be in the Lord,
I teach you today, even you."

Have you ever said, "I should have stayed in bed today.",
Because everything went the wrong way?
How did you start your day?
Did you take the time to pray?
Or were you in a hurry and a rush,
Stroking your hair with a brush?
We never know what we will face,
That's why we need God's strength to run the race.
Before we start each day,
Take time to pray,
And God's strength will uplift you all through the day.

Philippians 4:19

"And my God will meet all your needs
according to his glorious riches in Christ Jesus."

God's supply never runs out.
For it flows from His glorious riches, like water from a spout.
We are His children, and He will supply your needs.
Just trust Him, and you will see.

Matthew 6:33

"Seek first the kingdom of God and his righteousness, and all these things shall be added to you."

Would you say our basic need is food? Water? Shelter? Could it
be? Now all of these are a necessity.
But are they really our basic need?
Our most basic need is to be forgiven of our sins:
this is where life begins.
And as we trust God, don't you see,
He provides all of life's necessities.
Yes, He provides everything we need
We even have a home with Him, for eternity.

Luke 2:34-35

"Then Simeon blessed them and said to Mary, His mother:
this child is destined to cause the falling and rising of many in
Israel, and to be a sign that will be spoken against, so that the
thoughts of many hearts will be revealed and a sword pierce
your own soul too."

When Jesus came, many He would divide.
Some would accept Him, whiles others, Jesus they would deny.
His presence on earth brought rebuke to sin,
bringing out hearts of hostility that seem to never end.
The pain and suffering He would experience would affect others,
especially His mother.
What will we do with Jesus today?
Accept Him, or divided we stay.

Hebrews 4:16

"Let us therefore come boldly to the throne of grace that we
may obtain mercy and find grace to help in time of need."

God's grace do we understand,
It is Love that holds our hand.
His love and forgiveness is for every man,
Even if we can't understand.
When we accept His grace, He is in control.
We just have to trust Him, and be bold.
As He lives through us, we can say,
He touches other lives along the way.
There's no better feeling than to know,
We have a purpose and God loves us so.

Romans 8:39

"Neither height nor depth, nor anything else in all creation
will be able to separate us from the love of God that is in Christ
Jesus our Lord."

We all like to feel good about our self,
Especially when we help someone else.
How about when our patience runs thin,
And the words we use hurt someone within?
How do we feel and how does God look at us then?
No matter what we do, God will always love me and you.
He may not like our actions or our ways, but He loves us anyway.
We're something special don't you see, for He died for you and me.

Proverbs 16:24

"Pleasant words are as an honeycomb,
sweet to the soul, and health to the bones."

Words.
What we say
does it matter anyway?
They start in our heart and come through our mouth,
and sometimes that unkind word comes slipping out.
Words.
What we say can bring joy, or they can bring hurt
That leaves someone feeling like dirt.
How's that old saying go, that we heard long ago?
If you don't have something good to say,
you shouldn't say it anyway.

Luke 17:33

"Whoever tries to keep his life will lose it,
and whoever loses his life, will preserve it."

Be all you can be, that's what Jesus said.
Don't lie around like you are dead.
Get up, get out, and stir about.
You'll see God's up to something, there's no doubt.
Life can be dull or life can be fun,
But when you connect with Jesus,
You better be ready to run.
Happiness, joy and peace our life will be,
If we give it to Jesus,
The One who died for you and me.

Luke 2:20

"The shepherd's returned glorifying and praising God for all the things they had heard and seen, which were just as they had been told."

Once you meet Jesus, your life is not the same,
even though you return, from where you came,
you continue to glorify and praise His Holy name.

1 Thessalonians 2:4

"Our purpose is to please God, not people.
He is the one who examines the motives of our hearts."

Refuse to be defined by others,
This is our theme sisters and brothers.
Don't let the world squeeze you into its mold,
Simply let God take control.
Our minds the Lord will remold
And we will be complete and whole.
The plan of God is always good,
He works out things we never could.
Our purpose is to please Him alone,
Not Mary, Joe, Jim or Joan.
He knows the motives of our hearts,
So give it to Him, every part.
Yes, the world wants our heart,
But if we follow Jesus we will be smart.
And the world will see in us a changed heart.

Psalm 85:5

"You are forgiving and good, O Lord,
abounding in love to all who call to you."

Do your sins leave you feeling guilty, sad and blue?
Just remember God forgives through and through.
Jesus shed His blood on the cross, so our sins would be tossed.
Yes tossed, washed away!
Never again in our way
to hinder us, to make us blue,
to keep us from the one that loves me and you.
So lift your head, don't you sigh,
for we are forgiven by the One on high.

Proverbs 2:10-11

"For wisdom will enter your heart, and knowledge will be pleasant to your soul. Discretion will protect you, understanding will guard you."

When decisions we have to make,
It's God's wisdom we need to take.
Discernment to do what's right,
will lead us out of the dark and into the light

Matthew 2:3

"When King Herod heard this he was disturbed and all
Jerusalem with him."

The good news of Jesus does not bring joy to everyone,
for some it's a threat to remove them from their throne.
Yes, it's disturbing news they don't want to hear,
because of their sin, it causes great fear.

Psalm 107:8

"Let them give thanks to the Lord for His unfailing love and his
wonderful deeds for men."

Thanksgiving! What a wonderful day!
It is special in so many ways.
It's a time to reflect on God's great love,
and thank Him for all the blessings from above.
Time to spend with family and friends,
and oh what a joy to see all the smiles and grins.
A time to spend with our old feathered friend,
that's right, the ole turkey, and dressing and all the trimmings…let
the eating begin!
When the day is done and it's time to go,
we'll thank God for blessing us so.

CPSIA information can be obtained
at www.ICGtesting.com
Printed in the USA
LVOW04s0754090316

478337LV00002B/2/P

9 781498 464390